foundations

SMALL GROUP STUDY GUIDE

taught by tom Holladay and kay warren

THE AFTERLIFE

ZONDERVAN®

SADDLEBACK CHURCH

ZONDERVAN.com/
AUTHORTRACKER
follow your favorite authors

Foundations: *The Afterlife Study Guide*
Copyright © 2003, 2004, 2008 by Tom Holladay and Kay Warren

Requests for information should be addressed to:
Zondervan, *Grand Rapids, Michigan 49530*

ISBN 978-0-310-27689-0

FOREWORD

What *Foundations* Will Do for You

I once built a log cabin in the Sierra Mountains of northern California. After ten backbreaking weeks of clearing forest land, all I had to show for my effort was a leveled and squared concrete foundation. I was discouraged, but my father, who built over a hundred church buildings in his lifetime, said, "Cheer up, son! Once you've laid the foundation, the most important work is behind you." I've since learned that this is a principle for all of life: you can never build *anything* larger than the foundation can handle.

The foundation of any building determines both its size and strength, and the same is true of our lives. A life built on a false or faulty foundation will never reach the height that God intends for it to reach. If you skimp on your foundation, you limit your life.

That's why this material is so vitally important. *Foundations* is the biblical basis of a purpose-driven life. You must understand these life-changing truths to enjoy God's purposes for you. This curriculum has been taught, tested, and refined over ten years with thousands of people at Saddleback Church. I've often said that *Foundations* is the most important class in our church.

Why You Need a Biblical Foundation for Life

- *It's the source of personal growth and stability.* So many of the problems in our lives are caused by faulty thinking. That's why Jesus said the truth will set us free and why Colossians 2:7a (CEV) says, *"Plant your roots in Christ and let him be the foundation for your life."*

- *It's the underpinning of a healthy family.* Proverbs 24:3 (TEV) says, *"Homes are built on the foundation of wisdom and understanding."* In a world that is constantly changing, strong families are based on God's unchanging truth.

- **It's the starting point of leadership.** You can never lead people farther than you've gone yourself. Proverbs 16:12b (MSG) says, *"Sound leadership has a moral foundation."*

- **It's the basis for your eternal reward in heaven.** Paul said, *"Whatever we build on that foundation will be tested by fire on the day of judgment . . . We will be rewarded if our building is left standing"* (1 Corinthians 3:12, 14 CEV).

- **God's truth is the only foundation that will last.** The Bible tells us that *"the sound, wholesome teachings of the Lord Jesus Christ . . . are the foundation for a godly life"* (1 Timothy 6:3 NLT), and that *"God's truth stands firm like a foundation stone . . ."* (2 Timothy 2:19 NLT).

Jesus concluded his Sermon on the Mount with a story illustrating this important truth. Two houses were built on different foundations. The house built on sand was destroyed when rain, floods, and wind swept it away. But the house built on the foundation of solid rock remained firm. He concluded, *"Therefore everyone who hears these words of mine and puts them into practice is like a wise man who built his house on the rock"* (Matthew 7:24 NIV). *The Message* paraphrase of this verse shows how important this is: *"These words I speak to you are not incidental additions to your life . . . They are foundational words, words to build a life on."*

I cannot recommend this curriculum more highly to you. It has changed our church, our staff, and thousands of lives. For too long, too many have thought of theology as something that doesn't relate to our everyday lives, but *Foundations* explodes that mold. This study makes it clear that the foundation of what we do and say in each day of our lives is what we believe. I am thrilled that this in-depth, life-changing curriculum is now being made available for everyone to use.

— Rick Warren, author of *The Purpose Driven® Life*

PREFACE

Get ready for a radical statement, a pronouncement sure to make you wonder if we've lost our grip on reality: *There is nothing more exciting than doctrine!*

Track with us for a second on this. Doctrine is the study of what God has to say. What God has to say is always the truth. The truth gives me the right perspective on myself and on the world around me. The right perspective results in decisions of faith and experiences of joy. *That* is exciting!

The objective of *Foundations* is to present the basic truths of the Christian faith in a simple, systematic, and life-changing way—in other words, to teach doctrine. The question is, why? In a world in which people's lives are filled with crying needs, why teach doctrine? Because biblical doctrine has the answer to many of those crying needs! Please don't see this as a clash between needs-oriented and doctrine-oriented teaching. The truth is we need both. We all need to learn how to deal with worry in our lives. One of the keys to dealing with worry is an understanding of the biblical doctrine of the hope of heaven. Couples need to know what the Bible says about how to have a better marriage. They also need a deeper understanding of the doctrine of the Fatherhood of God, giving the assurance of God's love upon which all healthy relationships are built. Parents need to understand the Bible's practical insights for raising kids. They also need an understanding of the sovereignty of God, a certainty of the fact that God is in control, that will carry them through the inevitable ups and downs of being a parent. Doctrinal truth meets our deepest needs.

Welcome to a study that will have a lifelong impact on the way you look at everything around you and above you and within you. Helping you develop a "Christian worldview" is our goal as the writers of this study. A Christian worldview is the ability to see everything through the filter of God's truth. The time you dedicate to this study will lay a foundation for new perspectives that will have tremendous benefits for the rest of your life. This study will help you:

- Lessen the stress in everyday life

- See the real potential for growth the Lord has given you

- Increase your sense of security in an often troubling world

- Find new tools for helping others (your friends, your family, your children) find the right perspective on life

- Fall more deeply in love with the Lord

Throughout this study you'll see four types of sidebar sections designed to help you connect with the truths God tells us about himself, ourselves, and this world.

- *A Closer Look:* We'll take time to expand on a truth or look at it from a different perspective.

- *A Fresh Word:* One aspect of doctrine that makes people nervous is the "big words." Throughout this study we'll take a fresh look at these words, words like *omnipotent* and *sovereign.*

- *Key Personal Perspective:* The truth of doctrine always has a profound impact on our lives. In this section we'll focus on that personal impact.

- *Living on Purpose:* James 1:22 (NCV) says, *"Do what God's teaching says; when you only listen and do nothing, you are fooling yourselves."* In his book, *The Purpose Driven Life,* Rick Warren identifies God's five purposes for our lives. They are worship, fellowship, discipleship, ministry, and evangelism. We will focus on one of these five purposes in each lesson, and discuss how it relates to the subject of the study. This section is very important, so please be sure to leave time for it.

Here is a brief explanation of the other features of this study guide.

Looking Ahead/Catching Up: You will open each meeting with an opportunity for everyone to check in with each other about how you are doing with the weekly assignments. Accountability is a key to success in this study!

Key Verse: Each week you will find a key verse or Scripture passage for your group to read together. If someone in the group has a different translation, ask them to read it aloud so the group can get a bigger picture of the meaning of the passage.

Video Lesson: There is a video lesson segment for the group to watch together each week. Take notes in the lesson outlines as you watch the video, and be sure to refer back to these notes during your discussion time.

Discovery Questions: Each video segment is complemented by questions for group discussion. Please don't feel pressured to discuss every single question. The material in this study is meant to be your servant, not your master, so there is no reason to rush through the answers. Give everyone ample opportunity to share their thoughts. If you don't get through all of the discovery questions, that's okay.

Prayer Direction: At the end of each session you will find suggestions for your group prayer time. Praying together is one of the greatest privileges of small group life. Please don't take it for granted.

Get ready for God to do incredible things in your life as you begin the adventure of learning more deeply about the most exciting message in the world: the truth about God!

— Tom Holladay and Kay Warren

HOW TO USE THIS VIDEO CURRICULUM

Here is a brief explanation of the features on your small group DVD. These features include a *Group Lifter* by Tom Holladay, four *Video Teaching Sessions* by Kay Warren and a short video, *How to Become a Follower of Jesus Christ,* by Rick Warren. Here's how they work:

The Group Lifter is a brief video introduction by Tom Holladay giving you a sense of the objectives and purpose of this *Foundations* study on the afterlife. Watch it together as a group at the beginning of your first session.

The Video Teaching Sessions provide you with the teaching for each week of the study. Watch these features with your group. After watching the video teaching session, continue in your study by working through the discussion questions and activities in the study guide.

Nothing is more important than the decision you make to accept Jesus Christ as your Lord and Savior. You will have the option to watch a short video presentation, *How to Become a Follower of Jesus Christ,* at the end of Session Two. In this brief video segment, Rick Warren explains the importance of having Christ as the Savior of your life and how you can become part of the family of God. If everyone in your group is already a follower of Christ, or if you feel there is a better time to play this segment, continue your session by turning to the Discovery Questions in your DVD study guide. You can also select this video presentation separately on the Main Menu of the DVD for viewing at any time.

Follow these simple steps for a successful small group session:

1. Hosts: Watch the video session and write down your answers to the discussion questions in the study guide before your group arrives.

2. Group: Open your group meeting by using the "Looking Ahead" or "Catching Up" section of your lesson.

3. Group: Watch the video teaching lesson and follow along in the outlines in the study guide.

4. Group: Complete the rest of the discussion materials for each session in the study guide.

It's just that simple. Have a great study together!

1

Session One

HELL—A REAL PLACE

LOOKING AHEAD

What most strongly influenced your beliefs about the afterlife as you were growing up? What do you think influences most people's beliefs and opinions about the afterlife?

- The Bible
- Other world religions
- New Age thinking
- Wishful thinking
- Movies and television

Key Verse

... God has given us eternal life, and this life is in his Son. He who has the Son has life; he who does not have the Son of God does not have life.

1 John 5:11b–12 (NIV)

BIBLE TEACHING
Watch the video lesson now and take notes in your outline on pages 3–5.

Yes, a wise man thinks much of death, while the fool thinks only of having a good time now. (Ecclesiastes 7:4 LB)

Is Hell a Real Place?

Jesus taught that hell is a real place of judgment. In fact, there are more verses in which he taught about hell than about heaven.

> [24] *"Most assuredly, I say to you, he who hears My word and believes in Him who sent Me has everlasting life, and shall not come into judgment, but has passed from death into life.* [28] *... for the hour is coming in which all who are in the graves will hear His voice* [29] *and come forth—those who have done good, to the resurrection of life, and those who have done evil, to the resurrection of condemnation."* (John 5:24, 28–29 NKJV)

The Bible speaks of a time of judgment that all human beings will have to go through. It is referred to in several verses as being a time of "separating" or "sorting" the righteous from the unrighteous.

Verses	Metaphor
Matthew 13:47–51	A dragnet catching fish
Matthew 25:31–46	Shepherd sorting sheep and goats
Matthew 13:24–30	Harvester pulling weeds and wheat

Who is the one who judges and does the separating?

_____, the only righteous one, judges and does the separating.

For he has set a day for justly judging the world by the man he has appointed, and has pointed him out by bringing him back to life again. (Acts 17:31 LB)

Why Was Hell Created?

1. Hell was not created originally for any human being, but for
   _____ and his _____ .

   "Then he will say to those on his left, 'Depart from me, you who are cursed, into the eternal fire prepared for the devil and his angels.'" (Matthew 25:41 NIV)

2. Satan is not yet confined to hell. He now resides on _____ .

   "Now is the time for judgment on this world; now the prince of this world will be driven out." (John 12:31 NIV)

3. One day God is going to cast Satan, death, and Hades into the
   _____ .

   Then death and Hades were thrown into the lake of fire. The lake of fire is the second death. (Revelation 20:14 NIV)

Who Will Be in Hell?

Hell was created for Satan and the demons, but they will not be the only ones in hell for eternity.

The facts of life and eternity that we must all eventually face are:

1. We were all headed for an eternity _____ God in hell.

   All have sinned and are not good enough for God's glory. (Romans 3:23 NCV)

2. Jesus came to _____ us from separation from God.

> *. . . He is the one who has rescued us from the terrors of the coming judgment.* (1 Thessalonians 1:10b NLT)

3. Those who _____ Jesus are rescued!

> *Therefore he is able, once and forever, to save everyone who comes to God through him. He lives forever to plead with God on their behalf.* (Hebrews 7:25 NLT)

4. Those who do not trust Jesus are _____ rescued.

> *¹¹And this is the testimony: God has given us eternal life, and this life is in his Son. ¹²He who has the Son has life; he who does not have the Son of God does not have life.*
> (1 John 5:11–12 NIV)

KEY PERSONAL PERSPECTIVE
What about the people I love?

After we ourselves have been rescued from hell by trusting in the grace and love of Jesus, our minds immediately turn to those we love. The thought of their spending eternity separated from God is almost too painful for us to bear.

· If they're still living, don't give up _____ !

Let those you love know the good news that God can rescue them too. Many who initially reject God's invitation to life and forgiveness through Jesus end up accepting him.

· If they've already died, _____ them to God.

Remember that God is the ultimate judge of eternity; you are not. Instead of getting caught up in worrying about changing what you cannot change, leave it with God. Let your concern motivate you to share the hope that Jesus gives with those who are still living. And make sure that those you love have no doubt about your faith in Christ and the fact that you know you are going to heaven when you die.

DISCOVERY QUESTIONS

1. Why do you think the Bible so clearly and graphically tells us that hell is a place of suffering?

2. How does it make you feel to realize that you, as a Christian, will never have to stand before God to be judged on whether you'll be in heaven or hell? It's already settled!

3. What fears or insecurities still exist in your heart and mind regarding hell and eternal punishment? What can you do with these thoughts and feelings?

Did You Get It? How has this week's study helped you to see the reality of hell?

Share with Someone: Think of a person you can encourage with the truth you learned in this session. Write their name in the space below and pray for God to provide that opportunity this week.

LIVING ON PURPOSE
Evangelism

Who do you know who needs to hear the message of Jesus' sacrifice for them? You can use the *Circles of Life* diagram in the Small Group Resources section on page 44 to help identify those in your life who need to hear the gospel message. Begin to pray for an opportunity to share with them this week.

I will pray for God to prepare the hearts of and provide opportunities to speak to:

_____

I will make time this week to share Christ with: _____

PRAYER DIRECTION

Take some time as a group to talk about your specific prayer requests and to pray for one another. Ask God to reassure you concerning the truth about the afterlife and for boldness in sharing this truth with others.

Session two

2

THE TRUTH ABOUT HELL

CATCHING UP

Did you have an opportunity this week to tell anyone that Jesus is our rescuer? Is there someone you began to pray for on a more regular basis?

Key Verse

"Then they will go away to eternal punishment, but the righteous to eternal life."

Matthew 25:46 (NIV)

> **BIBLE TEACHING**
> Watch the video lesson now and take notes in your outline on pages 11–14.

What Happens to People in Hell?

"Then they will go away to eternal punishment, but the righteous to eternal life." (Matthew 25:46 NIV)

Three Kinds of Torment

- _____ torment

  "But the subjects of the kingdom will be thrown outside, into the darkness, where there will be weeping and gnashing of teeth." (Matthew 8:12 NIV)

- _____ torment

  [43] "So if your hand makes you lose your faith, cut it off! It is better for you to enter life without a hand than to keep both hands and go off to hell, to the fire that never goes out. [44, 45] And if your foot makes you lose your faith, cut it off! It is better for you to enter life without a foot than to keep both feet and be thrown into hell. [46, 47] And if your eye makes you lose your faith, take it out! It is better for you to enter the Kingdom of God with only one eye than to keep both eyes and be thrown into hell. [48] There 'the worms that eat them never die, and the fire that burns them is never put out.'" (Mark 9:43–48 GNT)

- _____ torment

  "Then he will say to those on his left, 'Depart from me, you who are cursed, into the eternal fire prepared for the devil and his angels.'" (Matthew 25:41 NIV)

They will be punished with everlasting destruction and shut out from the presence of the Lord and from the majesty of his power. (2 Thessalonians 1:9 NIV)

Where Do People Go Now When They Die?

The progressive revelation of the afterlife in the Bible

1. In the Old Testament, the afterlife was seen as a _____ and _____ place.

A FRESH WORD

Sheol

The Hebrew word *Sheol* is used sixty-six times in the Old Testament to refer to the place where a person's soul goes when they die. The earliest thoughts of Sheol indicate there was no distinction made in the minds of people between the morally good and the bad; all went to Sheol (Genesis 25:8; 37:35). As time went on, people began to believe that Sheol had sections; there was a contrast between the "lowest part" and the "highest part." While not clearly stated, it seems like the wicked are in the lowest part, while the righteous are in the highest part (Deuteronomy 32:22).

---

2. During the intertestamental period it was believed _____ had two distinct compartments.

   • One section was a place of torment for the wicked, called

     _____ .

   • The other was a place of conscious bliss, often called Abraham's

     bosom or _____ .

3. After Christ's resurrection:

- Believers who die enter into the presence of _____ .

- Unbelievers enter into a place of _____ .

The intermediate state and the resurrection of the body

> ⁶*Therefore we are always confident and know that as long as we are at home in the body we are away from the Lord.* ⁷*We live by faith, not by sight.* ⁸*We are confident, I say, and would prefer to be away from the body and at home with the Lord.* (2 Corinthians 5:6–8 NIV)

The "intermediate state" is the phrase used by theologians to describe the state that those who die are in between now and the time that Jesus comes again. Why the difference? Because while our souls go immediately to be with God or to suffer in Hades, our bodies have not yet been resurrected as Jesus' body was resurrected.

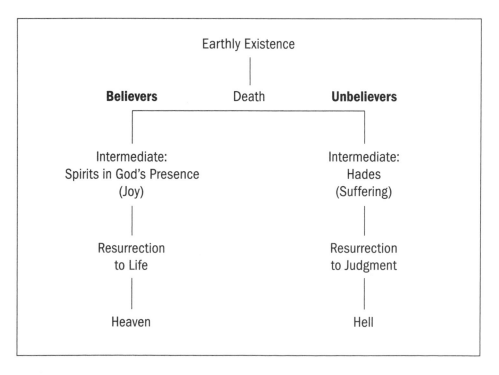

Earthly Existence

Believers Death **Unbelievers**

Intermediate: Intermediate:
Spirits in God's Presence Hades
(Joy) (Suffering)

Resurrection Resurrection
to Life to Judgment

Heaven Hell

KEY PERSONAL PERSPECTIVE

How can I be sure I won't spend eternity in hell?

What kind of horrible crime does a person have to commit to be sent to such a horrible place? Rejecting Jesus Christ as the Son of God, the Savior we all need, is the crime that will send a person to hell.

> [16]*"For God so loved the world that he gave his one and only Son, that whoever believes in him shall not perish but have eternal life.* [17]*For God did not send his Son into the world to condemn the world, but to save the world through him.* [18]*Whoever believes in him is not condemned, but whoever does not believe stands condemned already because he has not believed in the name of God's one and only Son."* (John 3:16-18 NIV)

Remember: If you decide (by desire or by neglect) to live separate form God in this life, you'll live separate from him in the next life. But if you accept God's offer of a relationship with him through Jesus in this life, you'll live with God in the next life!

"HOW TO BECOME A FOLLOWER OF JESUS CHRIST"

Have you ever surrendered your life to Jesus Christ? Take a few minutes with your group to watch a brief video by Pastor Rick Warren on how to become part of the family of God. It is included on the Main Menu of this DVD.

DISCOVERY QUESTIONS

1. Why should the concept of eternal separation from God be important to someone who has never had a relationship with God?

2. In the Bible, God assures us that when we die, we who are believers will immediately be in the presence of Jesus. How does this truth impact your heart?

3. Do you still have lingering doubts about what will happen to people you know and love after they die? Do you find it difficult to think about the eternal destiny of these people in light of what we are learning about the afterlife? How can your group support you in these doubts or concerns?

Did You Get It? How has this week's study helped you to see that God has always had a plan to rescue us from hell?

Share with Someone: Think of a person you can encourage with the truth you learned in this session. Write their name in the space below and pray for God to provide that opportunity this week.

LIVING ON PURPOSE
Ministry

Do you know a believer in Christ who needs reassurance that we will immediately be in the presence of Jesus when we die? Someone with doubts? Someone who is ill? Someone who has just lost a loved one? Write them a note or go see them this week, and talk with them about the promise from God's Word that your group studied together this week. Remember: we *all* need to be reminded of our assurance when going through difficult times!

PRAYER DIRECTION

Take some time together as a group to focus on two things:

- Giving praise for Jesus' willing sacrifice on the cross to save us from hell.

- Praying for those you know who have not yet trusted Christ to save them.

3

SESSION thREE

THE TRUTH ABOUT HEAVEN

CATCHING UP

In the last session we learned that rejecting Jesus Christ as the Savior is the crime that sends people to hell. We also saw that not only is hell a real place but suffering and separation from God is eternal if we fail to accept Jesus as our rescuer while we live here on earth. Did you have an opportunity this week to talk about these truths with anyone? How did the conversation go?

Key Verse

"I am telling you the truth: those who hear my words and believe in him who sent me have eternal life. They will not be judged, but have already passed from death to life."

John 5:24 (TEV)

BIBLE TEACHING
Watch the video lesson now and take notes in
your outline on pages 19–22.

Where Is Heaven?

Heaven is _____

> LORD, *I look up to you, up to heaven, where you rule.*
> (Psalm 123:1 GNT)

- Where the birds fly, the trees breathe, and the rain falls is
  referred to as the _____ heaven.
- Where the moon and stars move in their orbits is referred to as
  the _____ heaven.
- The _____ heaven, or highest heaven, is where God
  dwells in a special way.

Heaven is _____

- Heaven is _____ dwelling place and the _____
  dwelling place of believers.

  > *I heard a loud shout from the throne, saying, "Look, the
  > home of God is now among his people! He will live with them,
  > and they will be his people. God himself will be with them.*
  > (Revelation 21:3 NLT)

Who Will Be in Heaven?

> ²²*But you have come to Mount Zion, to the city of the living God, the heavenly Jerusalem. You have come to thousands of angels gathered together with joy.* ²³*You have come to the meeting of God's firstborn children whose names are written in heaven. You have come to God, the judge of all people, and to the spirits of good people who have been made perfect.* (Hebrews 12:22–23 NCV)

Those who will spend eternity with God are those who choose him in this life.

> *That if you confess with your mouth, "Jesus is Lord," and believe in your heart that God raised him from the dead, you will be saved.* (Romans 10:9 NIV)

A CLOSER LOOK
What about babies and children?

Will babies or children who die go to heaven? Yes! Although they are not old enough to be saved, they are kept safe by God's grace. A child (or someone who is mentally handicapped) who dies before reaching the age that they can understand their sin and need for Christ will not be held accountable for what they cannot understand. That would violate both God's justice and God's grace. Although the Bible does not directly answer this question, we can see two specific indications that the answer is yes:

1. God is just and righteous in everything he does.

   The LORD is righteous in all his ways and loving toward all he has made. (Psalm 145:17 NIV)

   He will not make a mistake in any of his judgments.

2. David believed that he would be reunited with his baby who had died (2 Samuel 12:23).

How Will I Be Judged as a Believer?

The Bible tells us of two times of judgment at the end of the world:

1. The _____ judgment

At this judgment, those who do not believe in Christ will hear their final judgment and sentencing of separation from God. Those who trust in Christ will not face this judgment.

> "I am telling you the truth: those who hear my words and believe in him who sent me have eternal life. They will not be judged, but have already passed from death to life."
> (John 5:24 TEV)

2. The _____ judgment

> For we must all appear before the judgment seat of Christ, that each one may receive what is due him for the things done while in the body, whether good or bad.
> (2 Corinthians 5:10 NIV)

The nature of the bema judgment

- What we've built into our lives that will last will be _____.
- What we've built into our lives that will not last will be _____.
- Whatever our rewards or loss, our salvation is _____.

> Therefore judge nothing before the appointed time; wait till the Lord comes. He will bring to light what is hidden in darkness and will expose the motives of men's hearts. At that time each will receive his praise from God. (1 Corinthians 4:5 NIV)

Believers will be rewarded for their:

1. _____

> "For the Son of Man is going to come in his Father's glory with his angels, and then he will reward each person according to what he has done." (Matthew 16:27 NIV)

2. _____

> "I the LORD search the heart and examine the mind, to reward a man according to his conduct, according to what his deeds deserve." (Jeremiah 17:10 NIV)

3. _____

> "But I tell you that men will have to give account on the day of judgment for every careless word they have spoken." (Matthew 12:36 NIV)

DISCOVERY QUESTIONS

1. There is no greater truth to build your life on, to reduce your anxieties, and to motivate you toward genuine greatness than the goal of heaven. How will your day look different if you live with heaven as the goal?

2. First Corinthians 3:10–15 says that believers who build the wrong things into their lives will "suffer loss" but will be saved. What do you think are some of the things that we build into our lives now that will be "burned up"? What are some of the things that will last?

3. How can your group encourage one another to live with eternity in mind? What are some practical ways you can develop a focus on heaven?

Did You Get It? How has this week's study helped you to see the reality of heaven?

Share with Someone: Think of a person you can encourage with the truth you learned in this session. Write their name in the space below and pray for God to provide that opportunity this week.

LIVING ON PURPOSE
Ministry

The reality of heaven should impact the value that we put upon ministry to others. We will be judged not on how much we owned, but on how we served God and ministered to others.

This week, ask God to enable you to value serving others, and thereby to choose serving others, in these three areas:

1. Your Actions
   In the way you act towards others.

2. Your Thoughts
   In the way you think about others—and pray for them.

3. Your Words
   In the words you say to others.

PRAYER DIRECTION

Take some time as a group to thank God for the reality of heaven and for the fact that you are headed there.

Session four

4

LIFE IN HEAVEN

CATCHING UP

1. How did the truth of heaven impact your daily life this past week? In what ways were you able to serve others through your thoughts, actions, and words?

2. Did you share with someone that Jesus is the only way to get into heaven? What was the result of your conversation?

Key Verse

Set your minds on things above, not on earthly things.

Colossians 3:2 (NIV)

BIBLE TEACHING
Watch the video lesson now and take notes in
your outline on pages 27–30.

What Will Heaven Be Like?

Six truths to bring you joy

> *You have made known to me the path of life; you will fill me
> with joy in your presence, with eternal pleasures at your right
> hand.* (Psalm 16:11 NIV)

1. There will be _____

> *And now, all glory to God, who is able to keep you from
> stumbling, and who will bring you into his glorious presence
> innocent of sin and with great joy.* (Jude 24 NLT)

> *Dear friends, now we are children of God, and we have not yet
> been shown what we will be in the future. But we know that
> when Christ comes again, we will be like him, because we will
> see him as he really is.* (1 John 3:2 NCV)

2. We will have _____ bodies

> *Now we know that if the earthly tent we live in is destroyed,
> we have a building from God, an eternal house in heaven, not
> built by human hands.* (2 Corinthians 5:1 NIV)

> *For while we are in this tent, we groan and are burdened,
> because we do not wish to be unclothed but to be clothed
> with our heavenly dwelling, so that what is mortal may be
> swallowed up by life.* (2 Corinthians 5:4 NIV)

3. _____

> *He will wipe away every tear from their eyes. There will be no more death or mourning or crying or pain, for the old order of things has passed away.* (Revelation 21:4 NIV)

> *For our earthly bodies, the ones we have now that can die, must be transformed into heavenly bodies that cannot perish but will live forever.* (1 Corinthians 15:53 LB)

4. _____ of all needs

> *Never again will they hunger; never again will they thirst. The sun will not beat upon them, nor any scorching heat.* (Revelation 7:16 NIV)

5. We share Christ's _____

> *Now if we are children, then we are heirs—heirs of God and co-heirs with Christ, if indeed we share in his sufferings in order that we may also share in his glory.* (Romans 8:17 NIV)

6. Intimate _____ with God and other believers

> *Now we see but a poor reflection as in a mirror; then we shall see face to face. Now I know in part; then I shall know fully, even as I am fully known.* (1 Corinthians 13:12 NIV)

How Can Heaven Affect My Life Now?

1. Motivation for _____

> *Jesus answered, "I am the way and the truth and the life. No one comes to the Father except through me."* (John 14:6 NIV)

[11] This is what God told us: God has given us eternal life, and this life is in his Son. [12] Whoever has the Son has life, but whoever does not have the Son of God does not have life. (1 John 5:11–12 NCV)

2. Wise use of _____

[19] "Don't store treasures for yourselves here on earth where moths and rust will destroy them and thieves can break in and steal them. [20] But store your treasures in heaven where they cannot be destroyed by moths or rust and where thieves cannot break in and steal them. [21] Your heart will be where your treasure is." (Matthew 6:19–21 NCV)

3. Serving the _____

[34] "Then the King will say to those on his right, 'Come, you who are blessed by my Father; take your inheritance, the kingdom prepared for you since the creation of the world. [35] For I was hungry and you gave me something to eat, I was thirsty and you gave me something to drink, I was a stranger and you invited me in, [36] I needed clothes and you clothed me, I was sick and you looked after me, I was in prison and you came to visit me.' [37] Then the righteous will answer him, 'Lord, when did we see you hungry and feed you, or thirsty and give you something to drink? [38] When did we see you a stranger and invite you in, or needing clothes and clothe you? [39] When did we see you sick or in prison and go to visit you?' [40] The King will reply, 'I tell you the truth, whatever you did for one of the least of these brothers of mine, you did for me.'" (Matthew 25:34–40 NIV)

4. Endurance in _____

[16] So we do not give up. Our physical body is becoming older and weaker, but our spirit inside us is made new every day. [17] We have small troubles for a while now, but they are helping us gain an eternal glory that is much greater than the troubles. [18] We set our eyes not on what we see but on what we cannot see. What we see will last only a short time, but what we cannot see will last forever. (2 Corinthians 4:16–18 NCV)

5. Easing of _____

> [1]*Since you became alive again, so to speak, when Christ arose from the dead, now set your sights on the rich treasures and joys of heaven where he sits beside God in the place of honor and power. [2]Let heaven fill your thoughts; don't spend your time worrying about things down here.* (Colossians 3:1–2 LB)

> *"Worthy is the Lamb, who was slain, to receive power and wealth and wisdom and strength and honor and glory and praise!"* (Revelation 5:12 NIV)

DISCOVERY QUESTIONS

1. As a group, brainstorm together for a few minutes about how great heaven will be by giving one-line completions to the following statements. Have fun with this!

   The greatest thing about heaven will be that I won't have to . . .

   The greatest thing about heaven will be that I will be able to . . .

   A picture that helps me to think of the greatness of heaven is . . .

   In heaven there will be an abundant supply of . . .

   In heaven there will be no . . .

Life IN HEAVEN

Someone I'm looking forward to meeting in heaven is . . .

Something I'm looking forward to doing in heaven is . . .

2. Look again at the six things that describe "what heaven will be like" on pages 27–28 of your outline notes. Which one sounds the most attractive to you right now? Which one is difficult to understand?

3. How would you like your glorified body to look? What would you like it to be able to do?

4. In what way would you like the truth of heaven to have a greater impact on your daily life?

Did You Get It? In what way has this week's study helped you see how the truth of heaven can make a difference in your everyday life?

Share with Someone: Think of a person you can encourage with the truth you learned in this session. Write their name in the space below and pray for God to provide that opportunity this week.

LIVING ON PURPOSE
Discipleship

God's Word repeatedly instructs us to shift our focus from earthly matters to God's perspective. Take a few minutes every day this week to reflect on the seven truths listed below. Consider where you may need a change in your thinking in order to live with eternity in view. Make yourself accountable to the group for growth in these areas.

- God's plan for me will never change.

- My salvation is safe and secure in heaven, where nothing can destroy it.

- When he comes for me I will go with him to the home he carefully and lovingly has been preparing for me.

- Nothing can ever separate me from his love—no pain, no suffering, no tragedy, no hardship, no demon, no horrible mistake on my part—nothing!

- I am to spend my days learning to love him and to trust him.

- I am to be his arms and hands of compassion to fellow human beings.

- Someday, I will join millions of other believers at his throne, and together we will worship him. We will sing with the angels, *"Worthy is the Lamb, who was slain, to receive power and wealth and wisdom and strength and honor and glory and praise!"* (Revelation 5:12 NIV)

PRAYER DIRECTION

Review the section of your outline notes, "How Can Heaven Affect My Life Now?" on pages 28–30 and read the verses listed there together. Check the areas below that you think are your areas of strength; then check the areas where you need to grow.

	Strengths	Growth Areas
Motivation for evangelism	❏	❏
Wise use of finances	❏	❏
Serving the needy	❏	❏
Endurance in suffering	❏	❏
Easing of anxieties	❏	❏

Now take some time to pray for each other, thanking God for areas of strength and asking for his power where you see you especially need to grow.

NOTES

Small Group Resources

HELPS FOR HOSTS

Top Ten Ideas for New Hosts

Congratulations! As the host of your small group, you have responded to the call to help shepherd Jesus' flock. Few other tasks in the family of God surpass the contribution you will be making.

As you prepare to facilitate your group, whether it is one session or the entire series, here are a few thoughts to keep in mind. We encourage you to read and review these tips with each new discussion host before he or she leads.

Remember you are not alone. God knows everything about you, and he knew you would be asked to facilitate your group. Even though you may not feel ready, this is common for all good hosts. God promises, *"I will never leave you; I will never abandon you"* (Hebrews 13:5 TEV). Whether you are facilitating for one evening, several weeks, or a lifetime, you will be blessed as you serve.

1. **Don't try to do it alone.** Pray right now for God to help you build a healthy team. If you can enlist a cohost to help you shepherd the group, you will find your experience much richer. This is your chance to involve as many people as you can in building a healthy group. All you have to do is ask people to help. You'll be surprised at the response.

2. **Be friendly and be yourself.** God wants to use your unique gifts and temperament. Be sure to greet people at the door with a big smile . . . this can set the mood for the whole gathering. Remember, they are taking as big a step to show up at your house as you are to lead this group! Don't try to do things exactly like another host; do them in a way that fits you. Admit when you don't have an answer and apologize when you make a mistake. Your group will love you for it and you'll sleep better at night.

3. **Prepare for your meeting ahead of time.** Review the session and write down your responses to each question. Pay special attention to exercises that ask group members to do something other than engage in discussion. These exercises will help your group live what the Bible teaches, not just talk about it. Be sure you understand how an exercise works. If the exercise employs one of the items in the Small Group Resources section (such as the Group Guidelines), be sure to look over that item so you'll know how it works.

4. **Pray for your group members by name.** Before you begin your session, take a few moments and pray for each member by name. You may want to review the prayer list at least once a week. Ask God to use your time together to touch the heart of every person in your group. Expect God to lead you to whomever he wants you to encourage or challenge in a special way. If you listen, God will surely lead.

5. **When you ask a question, be patient.** Someone will eventually respond. Sometimes people need a moment or two of silence to think about the question. If silence doesn't bother you, it won't bother anyone else. After someone responds, affirm the response with a simple "thanks" or "great answer." Then ask, "How about somebody else?" or "Would someone who hasn't shared like to add anything?" Be sensitive to new people or reluctant members who aren't ready to say, pray, or do anything. If you give them a safe setting, they will blossom over time. If someone in your group is a "wallflower" who sits silently through every session, consider talking to them privately and encouraging them to participate. Let them know how important they are to you—that they are loved and appreciated—and that the group would value their input. Remember, still water often runs deep.

6. **Provide transitions between questions.** Ask if anyone would like to read the paragraph or Bible passage. Don't call on anyone, but ask for a volunteer, and then be patient until someone begins. Be sure to thank the person who reads aloud.

7. **Break into smaller groups occasionally.** With a greater opportunity to talk in a small circle, people will connect more with the study, apply more quickly what they're learning, and ultimately get more out of their small group experience. A small circle also encourages a quiet person to participate and tends to minimize the effects of a more vocal or dominant member.

8. **Small circles are also helpful during prayer time.** People who are unaccustomed to praying aloud will feel more comfortable trying it with just two or three others. Also, prayer requests won't take as much time, so circles will have more time to actually pray. When you gather back with the whole group, you can have one person from each circle briefly update everyone on the prayer requests from their subgroups. The other great aspect of subgrouping is that it fosters leadership development. As you ask people in the group to facilitate discussion or to lead a prayer circle, it gives them a small leadership step that can build their confidence.

9. **Rotate facilitators occasionally.** You may be perfectly capable of hosting each time, but you will help others grow in their faith and gifts if you give them opportunities to host the group.

10. **One final challenge (for new or first-time hosts).** Before your first opportunity to lead, look up each of the six passages that follow. Read each one as a devotional exercise to help prepare you with a shepherd's heart. Trust us on this one. If you do this, you will be more than ready for your first meeting.

Matthew 9:36–38 (NIV)
36When Jesus saw the crowds, he had compassion on them, because they were harassed and helpless, like sheep without a shepherd. 37Then he said to his disciples, "The harvest is plentiful but the workers are few. 38Ask the Lord of the harvest, therefore, to send out workers into his harvest field."

John 10:14–15 (NIV)
14I am the good shepherd; I know my sheep and my sheep know me—15just as the Father knows me and I know the Father—and I lay down my life for the sheep.

1 Peter 5:2–4 (NIV)

²Be shepherds of God's flock that is under your care, serving as overseers—not because you must, but because you are willing, as God wants you to be; ³not greedy for money, but eager to serve; not lording it over those entrusted to you, but being examples to the flock. ⁴And when the Chief Shepherd appears, you will receive the crown of glory that will never fade away.

Philippians 2:1–5 (NIV)

¹If you have any encouragement from being united with Christ, if any comfort from his love, if any fellowship with the Spirit, if any tenderness and compassion, ²then make my joy complete by being like-minded, having the same love, being one in spirit and purpose. ³Do nothing out of selfish ambition or vain conceit, but in humility consider others better than yourselves. ⁴Each of you should look not only to your own interests, but also to the interests of others. ⁵Your attitude should be the same as that of Jesus Christ.

Hebrews 10:23–25 (NIV)

²³Let us hold unswervingly to the hope we profess, for he who promised is faithful. ²⁴And let us consider how we may spur one another on toward love and good deeds. ²⁵Let us not give up meeting together, as some are in the habit of doing, but let us encourage one another—and all the more as you see the Day approaching.

1 Thessalonians 2:7–8, 11–12 (NIV)

⁷. . . but we were gentle among you, like a mother caring for her little children. ⁸We loved you so much that we were delighted to share with you not only the gospel of God but our lives as well, because you had become so dear to us. . . . ¹¹For you know that we dealt with each of you as a father deals with his own children, ¹²encouraging, comforting and urging you to live lives worthy of God, who calls you into his kingdom and glory.

FREQUENTLY ASKED QUESTIONS

How long will this group meet?

This volume of *Foundations: The Afterlife* is four sessions long. We encourage your group to add a fifth session for a celebration. In your final session, each group member may decide if he or she desires to continue on for another study. At that time you may also want to do some informal evaluation, discuss your Group Guidelines, and decide which study you want to do next. We recommend you visit our website at **www.saddlebackresources.com** for more video-based small group studies.

Who is the host?

The host is the person who coordinates and facilitates your group meetings. In addition to a host, we encourage you to select one or more group members to lead your group discussions. Several other responsibilities can be rotated, including refreshments, prayer requests, worship, or keeping up with those who miss a meeting. Shared ownership in the group helps everybody grow.

Where do we find new group members?

Recruiting new members can be a challenge for groups, especially new groups with just a few people, or existing groups that lose a few people along the way. We encourage you to use the *Circles of Life* diagram on page 44 of this DVD study guide to brainstorm a list of people from your workplace, church, school, neighborhood, family, and so on. Then pray for the people on each member's list. Allow each member to invite several people from their list. Some groups fear that newcomers will interrupt the intimacy that members have built over time. However, groups that welcome newcomers generally gain strength with the infusion of new blood. Remember, the next person you add just might become a friend for eternity. Logistically, groups find different ways to add members. Some groups remain permanently open, while others choose to open periodically, such as at the beginning or end of a study. If your group becomes too large for easy, face-to-face conversations, you can subgroup, forming a second discussion group in another room.

How do we handle the child care needs in our group?

Child care needs must be handled very carefully. This is a sensitive issue. We suggest you seek creative solutions as a group. One common solution is to have the adults meet in the living room and share the cost of a babysitter (or two) who can be with the kids in another part of the house. Another popular option is to have one home for the kids and a second home (close by) for the adults. If desired, the adults could rotate the responsibility of providing a lesson for the kids. This last option is great with school-age kids and can be a huge blessing to families.

GROUP GUIDELINES

It's a good idea for every group to put words to their shared values, expectations, and commitments. Such guidelines will help you avoid unspoken agendas and unmet expectations. We recommend you discuss your guidelines during Session One in order to lay the foundation for a healthy group experience. Feel free to modify anything that does not work for your group.

We agree to the following values:

Clear Purpose	To grow healthy spiritual lives by building a healthy small group community
Group Attendance	To give priority to the group meeting (call if I am absent or late)
Safe Environment	To create a safe place where people can be heard and feel loved (no quick answers, snap judgments, or simple fixes)
Be Confidential	To keep anything that is shared strictly confidential and within the group
Conflict Resolution	To avoid gossip and to immediately resolve any concerns by following the principles of Matthew 18:15–17
Spiritual Health	To give group members permission to speak into my life and help me live a healthy, balanced spiritual life that is pleasing to God
Limit Our Freedom	To limit our freedom by not serving or consuming alcohol during small group meetings or events so as to avoid causing a weaker brother or sister to stumble (1 Corinthians 8:1–13; Romans 14:19–21)

GROUP GUIDELINES

Welcome Newcomers   To invite friends who might benefit from this study and warmly welcome newcomers

Building Relationships To get to know the other members of the group and pray for them regularly

Other   _____

We have also discussed and agreed on the following items:

Child Care

_____

_____

Starting Time

_____

Ending Time

_____

If you haven't already done so, take a few minutes to fill out the *Small Group Calendar* on page 48.

CIRCLES OF LIFE—SMALL GROUP CONNECTIONS

Discover who you can connect in community

Use this chart to help carry out one of the values in the Group Guidelines, to "Welcome Newcomers."

"Follow me, and I will make you fishers of men." (Matthew 4:19 KJV)

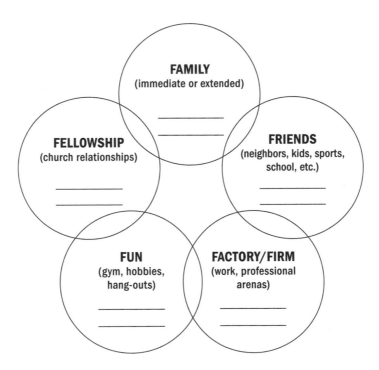

Follow this simple three-step process:

1. List 1–2 people in each circle.

2. Prayerfully select one person or couple from your list and tell your group about them.

3. Give them a call and invite them to your next meeting. Over 50 percent of those invited to a small group say, "Yes!"

SMALL GROUP PRAYER AND PRAISE REPORT

This is a place where you can write each other's requests for prayer. You can also make a note when God answers a prayer. Pray for each other's requests. If you're new to group prayer, it's okay to pray silently or to pray by using just one sentence: "God, please help

_____ to _____ ."

DATE	PERSON	PRAYER REQUEST	PRAISE REPORT

SMALL GROUP PRAYER AND PRAISE REPORT

DATE	PERSON	PRAYER REQUEST	PRAISE REPORT

SMALL GROUP PRAYER AND PRAISE REPORT

DATE	PERSON	PRAYER REQUEST	PRAISE REPORT

SMALL GROUP CALENDAR

Healthy groups share responsibilities and group ownership. It might take some time for this to develop. Shared ownership ensures that responsibility for the group doesn't fall to one person. Use the calendar to keep track of social events, mission projects, birthdays, or days off. Complete this calendar at your first or second meeting. Planning ahead will increase attendance and shared ownership.

DATE	LESSON	LOCATION	FACILITATOR	SNACK OR MEAL
5/4	Session 2	Chris and Andrea	Jim Brown	Phil and Karen

ANSWER KEY

Session One:
Hell—A Real Place

Jesus, the only righteous one, judges and does the separating.

1. Hell was not created originally for any human being, but for Satan and his angels.
2. Satan is not yet confined to hell. He now resides on Earth.
3. One day God is going to cast Satan, death, and Hades into the lake of fire.

1. We were all headed for an eternity without God in hell.
2. Jesus came to rescue us from separation from God.
3. Those who trust Jesus are rescued!
4. Those who do not trust Jesus are not rescued.

- If they're still living, don't give up hope!
- If they've already died, trust them to God.

Session Two:
The Truth about Hell

- Emotional torment
- Physical torment
- Spiritual torment

1. In the Old Testament, the afterlife was seen as a shadowy and unknown place.
2. During the intertestamental period it was believed Sheol had two distinct compartments.

- One section was a place of torment for the wicked, called Hades.
- The other was a place of conscious bliss, often called Abraham's bosom or Paradise.

- Believers who die enter into the presence of Christ.
- Unbelievers enter into a place of punishment.

Session Three:
The Truth about Heaven

Heaven is up

- Where the birds fly, the trees breathe, and the rain falls is referred to as the first heaven.
- Where the moon and stars move in their orbits i s referred to as the second heaven.
- The third heaven, or highest heaven, is where God dwells in a special way.

Heaven is home

- Heaven is God's dwelling place and the final dwelling place of believers.

1. The Great White Throne judgment
2. The "bema" judgment

- What we've built into our lives that will last will be rewarded.
- What we've built into our lives that will not last will be lost.
- Whatever our rewards or loss, our salvation is secure.

1. Actions
2. Thoughts
3. Words

Session Four:
Life in Heaven

1. There will be holiness
2. We will have glorified bodies
3. Immortality
4. Satisfaction of all needs
5. We share Christ's glory
6. Intimate fellowship with God and other believers

1. Motivation for evangelism
2. Wise use of finances
3. Serving the needy
4. Endurance in suffering
5. Easing of anxieties

NOTES

KEY VERSES

One of the most effective ways to drive deeply into our lives the principles we are learning in this series is to memorize key Scriptures. For many, memorization is a new concept or one that has been difficult in the past. We encourage you to stretch yourself and try to memorize these four key verses. If possible, memorize these as a group and make them part of your group time. You may cut these apart and carry them in your wallet.

I have hidden your word in my heart that I might not sin against you.

Psalm 119:11 (NIV)

Session One

*. . . God has given us eternal life,
and this life is in his Son.
He who has the Son has life;
he who does not have the Son
of God does not have life.*

1 John 5:11b–12 (NIV)

Session Two

*"Then they will go away to
eternal punishment, but the
righteous to eternal life."*

Matthew 25:46 (NIV)

Session Three

*"I am telling you the truth:
those who hear my words and
believe in him who sent me
have eternal life. They will not
be judged, but have already
passed from death to life."*

John 5:24 (TEV)

Session Four

*Set your minds on things above,
not on earthly things.*

Colossians 3:2 (NIV)

NOTES

We value your thoughts about what you've just read.
Please share them with us. You'll find contact information
in the back of this book.

The Purpose Driven® Life
A six-session video-based study for groups or individuals

Embark on a journey of discovery with this video-based study taught by Rick Warren. In it you will discover the answer to life's most fundamental question: "What on earth am I here for?"

And here's a clue to the answer: "It's not about you . . . You were created by God and for God, and until you understand that, life will never make sense. It is only in God that we discover our origin, our identity, our meaning, our purpose, our significance, and our destiny."

Whether you experience this adventure with a small group or on your own, this six-session, video-based study will change your life.

DVD Study Guide: 978-0-310-27866-5
DVD: 978-0-310-27864-1

Be sure to combine this study with your reading of the best-selling book, *The Purpose Driven® Life*, to give you or your small group the opportunity to discuss the implications and applications of living the life God created you to live.

Hardcover, Jacketed: 978-0-310-20571-5
Softcover: 978-0-310-27699-9

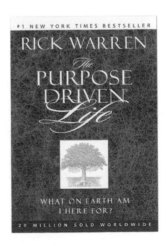

Pick up a copy today at your favorite bookstore!

ZONDERVAN®
.com

Foundations: 11 Core Truths to Build Your Life On

Taught by Tom Holladay and Kay Warren

Foundations is a series of 11 four-week video studies covering the most important, foundational doctrines of the Christian faith. Study topics include:

The Bible—This study focuses on where the Bible came from, why it can be trusted, and how it can change your life.

DVD Study Guide: 978-0-310-27670-8
DVD: 978-0-310-27669-2

God—This study focuses not just on facts about God, but on how to know God himself in a more powerful and personal way.

DVD Study Guide: 978-0-310-27672-2
DVD: 978-0-310-27671-5

Jesus—As we look at what the Bible says about the person of Christ, we do so as people who are developing a lifelong relationship with Jesus.

DVD Study Guide: 978-0-310-27674-6
DVD: 978-0-310-27673-9

The Holy Spirit—This study focuses on the person, the presence, and the power of the Holy Spirit, and how you can be filled with the Holy Spirit on a daily basis.

DVD Study Guide: 978-0-310-27676-0
DVD: 978-0-310-27675-3

Creation—Each of us was personally created by a loving God. This study does not shy away from the great scientific and theological arguments that surround the creation/evolution debate. However, you will find the goal of this study is deepening your awareness of God as your Creator.

DVD Study Guide: 978-0-310-27678-4
DVD: 978-0-310-27677-7

Pick up a copy today at your favorite bookstore!

ZONDERVAN®
.com

Salvation—This study focuses on God's solution to man's need for salvation, what Jesus Christ did for us on the cross, and the assurance and security of God's love and provision for eternity.

DVD Study Guide: 978-0-310-27682-1
DVD: 978-0-310-27679-1

Sanctification—This study focuses on the two natures of the Christian. We'll see the difference between grace and law, and how these two things work in our lives.

DVD Study Guide: 978-0-310-27684-5
DVD: 978-0-310-27683-8

Good and Evil—Why do bad things happen to good people? Through this study we'll see how and why God continues to allow evil to exist. The ultimate goal is to build up our faith and relationship with God as we wrestle with these difficult questions.

DVD Study Guide: 978-0-310-27687-6
DVD: 978-0-310-27686-9

The Afterlife—The Bible does not answer all the questions we have about what happens to us after we die; however, this study deals with what the Bible does tell us. This important study gives us hope and helps us move from a focus on the here and now to a focus on eternity.

DVD Study Guide: 978-0-310-27689-0
DVD: 978-0-310-27688-3

The Church—This study focuses on the birth of the church, the nature of the church, and the mission of the church.

DVD Study Guide: 978-0-310-27692-0
DVD: 978-0-310-27691-3

The Second Coming—This study addresses both the hope and the uncertainties surrounding the second coming of Jesus Christ.

DVD Study Guide: 978-0-310-27695-1
DVD: 978-0-310-27693-7

Pick up a copy today at your favorite bookstore!

ZONDERVAN®
.com

Celebrate Recovery, Updated Curriculum Kit

This kit will provide your church with the tools necessary to start a successful Celebrate Recovery program. *Kit includes:*

- Introductory Guide for Leaders DVD
- Leader's Guide
- 4 Participant's Guides (one of each guide)
- CD-ROM with 25 lessons
- CD-ROM with sermon transcripts
- 4-volume audio CD sermon series

Curriculum Kit: 978-0-310-26847-5

Participant's Guide 4-pack

The Celebrate Recovery Participant's Guide 4-pack is a convenient resource when you're just getting started or if you need replacement guides for your program.

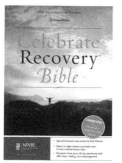

Celebrate Recovery Bible

With features based on eight principles Jesus voiced in his Sermon on the Mount, the new *Celebrate Recovery Bible* offers hope, encouragement, and empowerment for those struggling with the circumstances of their lives and the habits they are trying to control.

Hardcover: 978-0-310-92849-2
Softcover: 978-0-310-93810-1

Pick up a copy today at your favorite bookstore!

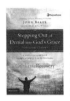

Stepping Out of Denial into God's Grace

Participant's Guide 1 introduces the eight principles of recovery based on Jesus' words in the Beatitudes, and focuses on principles 1–3. Participants learn about denial, hope, sanity, and more.

Getting Right with God, Yourself, and Others

Participant's Guide 3 covers principles 5–7 based on Jesus' words in the Beatitudes. With courage and support from their fellow participants, people seeking recovery will find victory, forgiveness, and grace.

Taking an Honest and Spiritual Inventory

Participant's Guide 2 focuses on the fourth principle based on Jesus' words in the Beatitudes and builds on the Scripture, *"Happy are the pure in heart."* (Matthew 5:8) The participant will learn an invaluable principle for recovery and also take an in-depth spiritual inventory.

Growing in Christ While Helping Others

Participant's Guide 4 walks through the final steps of the eight recovery principles based on Jesus' words in the Beatitudes. In this final phase, participants learn to move forward in newfound freedom in Christ, learning how to give back to others. There's even a practical lesson called "Seven reasons we get stuck in our recoveries."

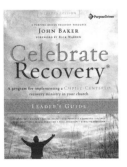

Leader's Guide

The Celebrate Recovery Leader's Guide gives you everything you need to facilitate your preparation time. Virtually walking you through every meeting, the Leader's Guide is a must-have for every leader on your Celebrate Recovery ministry team.

Pick up a copy today at your favorite bookstore!

ZONDERVAN®
.com

Wide Angle:
Framing Your Worldview

Christianity is much more than a religion. It is a worldview—a way of seeing all of life and the world around you. Your worldview impacts virtually every decision you make in life: moral decisions, relational decisions, financial decisions—everything. How you see the world determines how you face the world.

In this brand new study, Rick Warren and Chuck Colson discuss such key issues as moral relativism, tolerance, terrorism, creationism vs. Darwinism, sin and suffering. They explore in depth the Christian worldview as it relates to the most important questions in life:

- Why does it matter what I believe?
- How do I know what's true?
- Where do I come from?
- Why is the world so messed up?
- Is there a solution?
- What is my purpose in life?

Rick Warren   *Chuck Colson*

This study is as deep as it is wide, addressing vitally important topics for every follower of Christ.

DVD Study Guide: 978-1-4228-0083-6
DVD: 978-1-4228-0082-9

The Way of a Worshiper

The pursuit of God is the chase of a lifetime—in fact, it's been going on since the day you were born. The question is: Have you been the hunter or the prey?

This small group study is not about music. It's not even about going to church. It's about living your life as an offering of worship to God. It's about tapping into the source of power to live the Christian life. And it's about discovering the secret to friendship with God.

In these four video sessions, Buddy Owens helps you unpack the meaning of worship. Through his very practical, engaging, and at times surprising insights, Buddy shares truths from Scripture and from life that will help you understand in a new and deeper way just what it means to be a worshiper.

God is looking for worshipers. His invitation to friendship is open and genuine. Will you take him up on his offer? Will you give yourself to him in worship? Then come walk *The Way of a Worshiper* and discover the secret to friendship with God.

DVD Study Guide: 978-1-4228-0096-6
DVD: 978-1-4228-0095-9

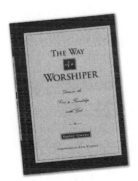

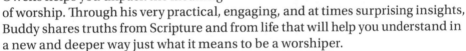

THE WAY of a WORSHIPER

Your study of this material will be greatly enhanced by reading the book, *The Way of a Worshiper: Discover the Secret to Friendship with God.*

Managing Our Finances God's Way

Did you know that there are over 2,350 verses in the Bible about money? Did you know that nearly half of Jesus' parables are about possessions? The Bible is packed with wise counsel about your financial life. In fact, Jesus had more to say about money than about heaven and hell combined.

Introducing a new video-based small group study that will inspire you to live debt free! Created by Saddleback Church and Crown Financial Ministries, learn what the Bible has to say about our finances from Rick Warren, Chip Ingram, Ron Blue, Howard Dayton, and Chuck Bentley as they address important topics like:

- God's Solution to Debt
- Saving and Investing
- Plan Your Spending
- Giving as an Act of Worship
- Enjoy What God Has Given You

Study includes:

- DVD with seven 20-minute lessons

- Workbook with seven lessons

- Resource CD with digital version of all worksheets that perform calculations automatically

- Contact information for help with answering questions

- Resources for keeping financial plans on track and making them lifelong habits

NOTE: PARTICIPANTS DO NOT SHARE PERSONAL FINANCIAL INFORMATION WITH EACH OTHER.

DVD Study Guide: 978-1-4228-0083-6
DVD: 978-1-4228-0082-9

TO ORDER PRODUCT OR FOR MORE INFORMATION:
www.saddlebackresources.com or call 1.800.723.3532

Share Your Thoughts

With the Author: Your comments will be forwarded to the author when you send them to *zauthor@zondervan.com*.

With Zondervan: Submit your review of this book by writing to *zreview@zondervan.com*.

Free Online Resources at
www.zondervan.com/hello

 Zondervan AuthorTracker: Be notified whenever your favorite authors publish new books, go on tour, or post an update about what's happening in their lives.

 Daily Bible Verses and Devotions: Enrich your life with daily Bible verses or devotions that help you start every morning focused on God.

 Free Email Publications: Sign up for newsletters on fiction, Christian living, church ministry, parenting, and more.

 Zondervan Bible Search: Find and compare Bible passages in a variety of translations at www.zondervanbiblesearch.com.

 Other Benefits: Register yourself to receive online benefits like coupons and special offers, or to participate in research.